Dedicated to Lodie, Louis and Owen.

Special thanks to Robyn Farber.

Copyright © 2024 Durand Loy
All rights reserved.

ISBN 979-8-9901884-0-2 (paperback)
ISBN 979-8-9901884-1-9 (hardback)
ISBN 979-8-9901884-2-6 (e-book)

Written by Durand Loy
Illustrations by Ayan Mansoori

Published by Durand Books
Visit www.durandbooks.com

THE STORIES OF
The Bible
AN INSPIRING CHRISTIAN STORYBOOK FOR KIDS

Written by Durand Loy

Illustrated by Ayan Mansoori

creation
(Genesis 1:1 - 2:2)

In the beginning, God made everything by speaking. He said "let there be light", and there was light! He created the land, seas, and all of the animals. On the sixth day, God made Adam and Eve, the first people, and put them in a lovely place called the Garden of Eden. This story shows how amazing God's power is and how much He loves everything He made.

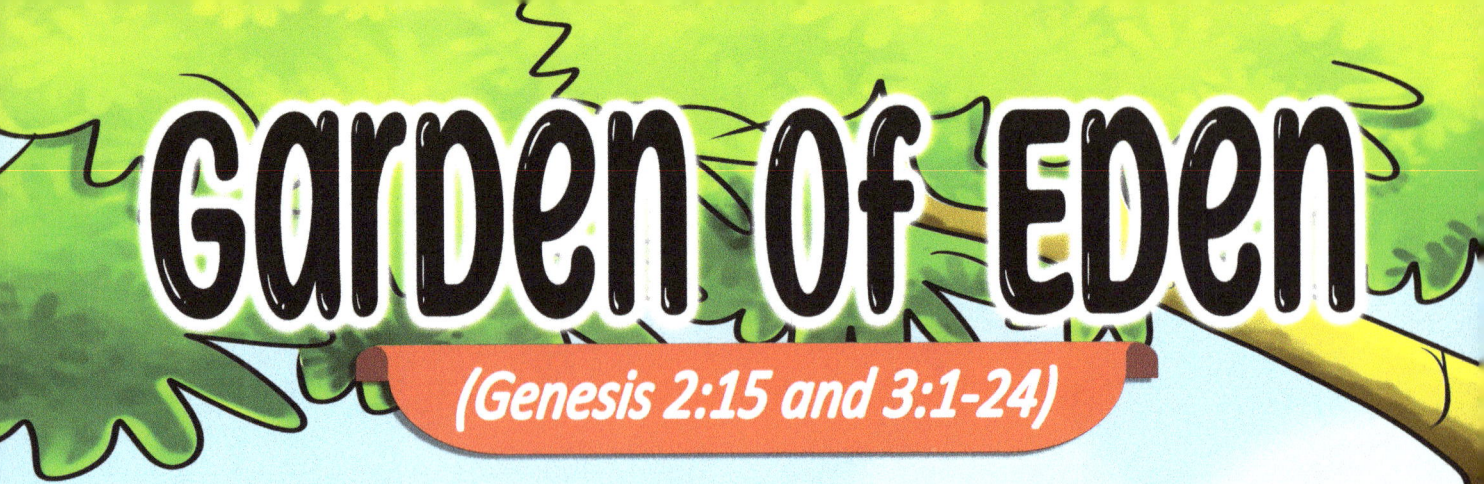

Garden of Eden
(Genesis 2:15 and 3:1-24)

In a beautiful garden called Eden, there lived a man named Adam and his wife named Eve. They had a special job to take care of the garden. One day, they made a big mistake and listened to a lying snake that tricked them into eating fruit from a tree that God told them to never eat from. Because of this, they had to leave the garden. God still loved them and promised to take care of them.

Noah's Ark
(Genesis 9:12-17)

God told Noah to build a big boat called an ark because He was going to send flood waters to cover the earth. Noah obeyed God and built the ark. Next, he brought two of every kind of animal onto the ark with him. It rained and rained, but Noah and the animals were safe on the ark. When the rain stopped, God dried up the land, and He sent a rainbow as a promise that He would never flood the earth again.

Joseph and His Colorful Coat

(Genesis 37:1-36)

Joseph was his father's favorite and got a special coat with many colors. His brothers felt jealous and sold him as a slave. But Joseph's story is about never giving up, forgiving others, and how God has a plan for all of us.

Moses and the Burning Bush

(Exodus 3:1-20)

There once was a man named Moses. One day, he was taking care of his sheep when something amazing happened! He saw a bush that was on fire but not burning up! God spoke to Moses from the bush and asked him to help lead the Israelites, God's special people, out of slavery in Egypt. Moses listened to God and became a great leader who helped his people.

Red Sea Crossing

(Exodus 14:16-31)

Moses led the Israelites out of Egypt to escape slavery. When they came to the Red Sea, they had no way to cross it. So, God did something incredible! He told Moses to raise up his staff and stretch his hand over the sea to divide the water. This would give the Israelites a way to cross the sea on dry land. After they crossed safely, God told Moses to stretch out his hand again to make the water flow back together so the Egyptians could not follow them!

The Ten Commandments

(Exodus 20:1-17)

God gave Moses the Ten Commandments to teach His people how to live in a way that pleases Him. These commandments include things like loving God, respecting parents, being honest, and not hurting others. They help us know how to live in a way that makes God happy and keeps us safe.

The Battle of Jericho

(Joshua 6:1-16)

Joshua led the Israelites around the walls of Jericho. When they shouted, the walls fell down! It was a big victory, showing that with faith, even the hardest things can be overcome with God's help.

Samson Pushing Down Columns

(Judges 16:23-31)

Samson was a very strong man because God gave him special strength like no other man on earth. Even though Samson was strong, he wasn't always wise. One day, he was captured and put into prison by his enemies. They blinded him and made fun of him and Samson lost all of his strength. Samson continued to pray to God, he asked God to help him be strong and courageous one last time. One day, while no one was looking, with all his might, he pushed down big columns that made their temple and their false gods fall down! In the end, Samson showed his enemies how powerful faith in God can be.

Deborah the Prophet

(Judges 4)

Deborah was a Prophet and Judge over Israel in the time before Kings. God chose Deborah because she was wise. She held court under a palm tree, and the Israelites would come to her when they needed help because she always knew what to do. One day Deborah told Barak, a strong warrior, to gather an army of 10,000 men to defeat the Canaanites. Barak hesitated and said, "I'll obey if you will go with me!" So Deborah went with Barak to the battle ground. With Deborah's guidance Barak led the Israelites to victory just like God promised! The land had peace for forty years under Deborah's leadership, and the people praised God for her wisdom and courage.

David and Goliath

(1 Samuel 17:1-50)

There once was a big, scary giant named Goliath, and a small boy named David. Even though David was small, he trusted in God and fought Goliath with just a sling and a stone. With God's help, David won the battle against Goliath and showed us that even the smallest person can do big things with faith.

Daniel in the Lion's Den

(Daniel 6:1-23)

Daniel loved to pray to God every day. But one day, some people didn't like that, so they threw him into a den full of hungry lions. God protected Daniel! He sent an angel to shut the lions' mouths so they couldn't hurt him. When the king saw that Daniel was safe, he praised God, and Daniel continued to pray every day.

Jonah and the Whale

(Jonah 1:1-3:6)

God told Jonah to go to a city called Nineveh and tell the people to stop doing bad things. But Jonah didn't want to listen to God, so he ran away to hide. He got on a ship to sail far away when a big storm came! Jonah told the sailors to throw him overboard into the sea to save the ship from sinking! And as they did, a big fish swallowed Jonah up! Inside the fish, Jonah prayed to God to ask forgiveness for running away. After three days, the fish spit him out on the shore. Jonah then went to Nineveh and told the people about God.

The Birth of Jesus

(Luke 2: 1-20)

In Bethlehem, Mary gave birth to a baby named Jesus. Angels sang in the sky, and shepherds came to visit. The angels sang, "Glory to God in the highest heaven, and on earth, peace to those on whom his favor rests."

The Three Wise Men

(Matthew 2:1-12)

Three wise men from far away saw a bright star in the sky. They followed it and found baby Jesus in Bethlehem. They brought him gifts of gold, frankincense, and myrrh. They knew Jesus was the child of God and wanted to honor him.

Jesus Feeds 5000 People

(Matthew 14:13-21)

One day, Jesus was teaching a large crowd of people on a hill. They had been there all day and were getting very hungry. There wasn't enough food for so many people, but Jesus wasn't worried. He blessed five small loaves of bread and two fish. Miraculously, He multiplied the food so everyone could eat. They even had leftovers! This showed them Jesus was the Son of God and could provide for the needs of all people.

Jesus Walks on Water

(Matthew 14:22-33)

One stormy night, Jesus' disciples were in a boat on a rough sea. Suddenly, they saw Jesus walking towards them on the water! They thought he was a ghost! But Jesus said, "Don't be afraid"! The disciple, Peter, asked Jesus to tell him to walk on the water. And he did! The disciples could see that Jesus had power over everything! They never had to be afraid with Jesus by their side!

The Mustard Seed

(Matthew 17:20)

Jesus said that the kingdom of heaven is like a tiny mustard seed that grows into a big tree. Even though the seed is very small, it grows and becomes a place where birds can make nests. Jesus meant that even small acts of faith and kindness can grow and make a big difference in the world.

The Healing of Blind Bartimaeus

(Mark 10:46-52)

Bartimaeus was a blind man, and he sat by the road, begging for help. When he heard that Jesus was passing by, he called out to Him, "Jesus, have mercy on me!" Jesus heard him and healed his eyes. Bartimaeus was so happy, and he followed Jesus, thanking Him for giving him the gift of sight.

Jesus Calming the Storm

(Mark 4:35-41)

One night Jesus and his disciples were in a boat crossing the sea when a huge storm came. The storm created big waves that almost sank the boat. But Jesus told the sea, "Peace! Be still!", and the storm stopped! This story shows how Jesus has power over everything, even the scariest storms. It reminds us to trust Him no matter what happens.

THE GOOD SAMARITAN

(Luke 10:25-37)

Once, there was hurt man lying on the side of the road. Many busy people passed by him and didn't bother to stop and help. Along came a kind man from Samaria who felt sorry for the man. He decided to take action and take him to the doctor. This Good Samaritan showed love and kindness to a man who had no one else to help him. This act of kindness teaches us that helping others is the right thing to do.

Parable of the Lost Sheep

(Luke 15:1-7)

Jesus told a story about a shepherd who had one hundred sheep. One day, one of the sheep wandered away. The shepherd left the other ninety-nine sheep and went to look for the lost one. When he found it, he was so happy! Jesus said that in the same way, God is like the shepherd who searches for and cares for each and every one of us.

The Prodigal Son

(Luke 15:11-32)

There was a man who had two sons. The younger son asked his father for his share of the family's money and went far away to another city. While he was there, he spent all of it! He soon had no money left for food or water. He realized he had made a big mistake by taking the family's money and spending it all on himself! He was so sad that he decided to go back to his father and tell him he was sorry. His father welcomed him home with open arms and forgave him because a father loves his children no matter what.

Palm Sunday

(John 12: 12-15)

On Palm Sunday, Jesus rode into Jerusalem on a donkey. The people welcomed Him by waving palm branches and shouting, "Hosanna!" They laid their cloaks and palm branches on the road for Jesus to ride over. It was a special day because the people recognized Jesus as their King.

The Last Supper
(John 13)

Before Jesus was crucified on the cross, he had a special dinner with his disciples. During the meal, He told them that He loved them and shared bread and wine with them. He asked them to remember him always. He also told them of his plan to die on the cross for their sins. He did this so that they all could be together in heaven one day!

The Resurrection
(John 20:1-18)

After Jesus died, his followers were very sad. But on the third day, something amazing happened! Jesus came back to life! He showed himself to his friends, and they were filled with joy! Jesus died and rose from the dead to prepare a place for us in heaven! He is our Savior now and always.

Paul's Shipwreck

(Acts 27:1-44)

Paul was traveling on a ship when a big storm came. The ship was in danger of sinking, but Paul trusted in God and told the people not to worry. An angel appeared to Paul and promised him that everyone on the ship would be safe. The ship eventually crashed into an island, but everyone made it safely to shore because God protected them.

THE ARMOR OF GOD

(Ephesians 6:10-16)

God provides us strength. He knows that we need to be strong and protected, so God gave us armor. He gave us a belt of truth, breastplate of righteousness, shoes of peace, shield of faith, helmet of salvation, and a sword of the Spirit. With God's armor, we are strong and brave, ready to face anything that comes our way.

FREE Coloring Pages!

If you enjoyed this book, you'll love our coloring books!
Check them out for FREE by scanning the QR Code below!

About the Author

Durand Loy, a native of Natchez, Mississippi, is an author deeply committed to crafting enriching literary experiences for children of all ages. Born and raised in the heart of the South, Durand draws inspiration from his Southern roots and family life as a devoted husband and father of two young boys.

With a passion for instilling strong moral and ethical values in children, Durand specializes in creating faith-based children's books and engaging coloring books. His works are not only educational but also serve as tools for fostering character development and spiritual growth in young readers.

Driven by his belief in the power of storytelling, Durand endeavors to make learning and reading enjoyable experiences for children. Through his books, he seeks to spark curiosity, encourage empathy, and promote understanding, all while imparting valuable life lessons.

Durand Loy's dedication to creating uplifting and wholesome literature reflects his unwavering commitment to nurturing the minds and hearts of the next generation. With each page turn, he invites readers on a journey of imagination, discovery, and, above all, the celebration of love, faith, and family values.

A Note From the Author

Dear Readers,

I'm writing to express my gratitude for your support and to kindly request a small favor.

Reviews on platforms like Amazon play a crucial role in helping potential readers discover new books. Your honest opinion could be the deciding factor for someone on the fence about picking up one of my books.

If you found this book to be engaging and fun, please consider taking a moment to share your thoughts on Amazon. Your review doesn't need to be lengthy; even a few words about what resonated with you would be immensely valuable.

Your feedback not only helps other readers but also provides me with invaluable insight into what aspects of my publications are working well and where there may be room for improvement.

Thank you for considering my request, and thank you once again for your support of my work. Your support means the world to me.

Please scan the QR code below to find all of my books in one place on Amazon.com.

Warm regards,
Durand

Let's Stay Connected!

Scan the QR code below to learn more about us at Durandbooks.com

Scan the QR code below to follow me on Facebook!

www.ingramcontent.com/pod-product-compliance
Lightning Source LLC
Chambersburg PA
CBHW061405010526
44119CB00010B/262